UNDER
THE
METAL
MAN

UNDER
THE
METAL
MAN
SLIGO IN YEATS

JOSEPH M. HASSETT

THE LILLIPUT PRESS • DUBLIN • MMXXIV

First published 2024 by
THE LILLIPUT PRESS
62–63 Sitric Road, Arbour Hill
Dublin 7, Ireland
www.lilliputpress.ie

ISBN 978 1 84351 884 6

A CIP record for this title is available
from The British Library.

10 9 8 7 6 5 4 3 2 1

Set in 11.5 pt on 16 pt Fournier by iota (iota-books.ie)
Printed by Finidr, Czech Republic

Sligo in Yeats

This book brings together images of books and visual art that reflect Sligo's presence in the work of W.B. Yeats and the Yeats family. Most of the objects depicted in the book are contained in a collection donated to Yeats Society Sligo.

Sligo vibrates at the heart of Yeats's work. His poetry bears out the assertion in his draft autobiography that 'In a sense Sligo has always been my home.' One could almost say of his writing what his brother Jack wrote of his painting: 'every painting which I have made has somewhere in it a thought of Sligo'.

We can learn a lot about Yeats in Sligo and Sligo in Yeats from the material objects in the collection. They are part of what Henry James called 'the visitable past' – a realm 'fragrant of … the poetry of the thing outlived

... and yet in which the precious element of closeness, telling so of connexions but tasting so of differences, remains appreciable'.

Some of the books are an especially resonant part of the visitable past because they bear inscriptions, and thus contain a tangible trace of their author. As poet Susan Howe explained in a comment on the subject of her book *Spontaneous Particulars: The Telepathy of Archives*, 'the piece of paper ... is all we have to connect with the dead ... There's a level at which words are spirit and paper is skin. That's the fascination of archives. There's still a bodily trace.'

Other objects in the collection evoke the visitable past in their own distinctive way. The beautiful Cuala Press first editions are imbued with Elizabeth ('Lolly') Yeats's extraordinary talent for typesetting and design, and embody her commitment to making books that are permanent works of art – fitting companions to her brother's poetry. Lolly's *Brush-Work Studies* is shown and discussed in chapter 12.

All of the objects in the collection show us what it was to experience the poetry and art contemporaneously with its creation, thus carrying us to the visitable past and inviting exploration of the relationship between Sligo and works of genius created by the Yeats family.

RESPONSIBILITIES: POEMS AND A
PLAY BY WILLIAM BUTLER YEATS

THE CUALA PRESS
CHURCHTOWN
DUNDRUM
MCMXIV

Pardon, old fathers, if you still remain
Somewhere in ear-shot for the story's end,
Old Dublin merchant 'free of ten and four'
Or trading out of Galway into Spain;
And country scholar, Robert Emmet's friend,
A hundred-year-old memory to the poor;
Traders or soldiers who have left me blood
That has not passed through any huxter's loin,
Pardon, and you that did not weigh the cost,
Old Butlers when you took to horse and stood
Beside the brackish waters of the Boyne
Till your bad master blenched and all was lost;
And merchant skipper that leaped overboard
After a ragged hat in Biscay Bay,
You most of all, silent and fierce old man
Because you were the spectacle that stirred
My fancy, and set my boyish lips to say
'Only the wasteful virtues earn the sun;'
Pardon that for a barren passion's sake,
Although I have come close on forty-nine
I have no child, I have nothing but a book,
Nothing but that to prove your blood and mine.

January, 1914.

Responsibilities (Cuala Press, 1914): title page and introductory rhyme

In his essay about Yeats and the place of writing Seamus Heaney suggests that there are two types of relationship between writer and place. In one, the writer gives voice to the spirit of the region. In the other, the writer has a more domineering relationship to the physical world, and the writing creates a country of the mind rather than the other way round. He cites Hardy and the young Yeats as examples of the first relationship, and Yeats from age fifty on as an example of the second.

Interestingly, in this first piece of the visitable past in the collection, Yeats makes a point of the fact that he is almost forty-nine years old, on the cusp of the age where Heaney detects a turning point in Yeats's relationship to place. In these introductory rhymes, Yeats plants himself firmly in a line of Sligo ancestors. The poet seeks the pardon of his 'old fathers' for his having 'come close on forty-nine' but having 'no child, ... nothing but a book, ... to prove your blood and mine'. Chief among the old fathers addressed is Yeats's maternal grandfather, Sligo man William Pollexfen, that 'silent and fierce old man', whose 'spectacle ... stirred / My fancy, and set my boyish lips to say / "Only the wasteful virtues earn the sun"'.

In *Reveries Over Childhood and Youth* Yeats sheds light on the nature of the 'wasteful virtues' by describing the spectacle that stirred his fancy. He tells us that his grandfather

> had great physical strength and had the reputation of never ordering a man to do anything he would not

do himself. He owned many sailing-ships and once, when a captain just come to anchor at Rosses Point reported something wrong with the rudder, had sent a messenger to say, 'Send a man down to find out what's wrong'. 'The crew all refuse', was the answer, and to that my grandfather answered, 'Go down yourself', and that not being obeyed, he dived from the main deck, all the neighbourhood lined along the pebbles of the shore. He came up with his skin torn but well informed about the rudder. He had a violent temper and kept a hatchet at his bedside for burglars ... Even to-day when I read *King Lear* his image is always before me, and I often wonder if the delight in passionate men in my plays and in my poetry is more than his memory.

The spectacle of William Pollexfen risking injury to repair the rudder under the gaze of his neighbours fixed itself firmly in Yeats's mind. The carefully recounted details suggest that wasteful virtues are characterized by recklessness and extravagance. Significantly, Yeats had used both of these words in discussing the quality of *sprezzatura* that he admired when Augusta Gregory read him Thomas Hoby's translation of Castiglione's *The Book of the Courtier*. Hoby translated the courtier's characteristic attribute of *sprezzatura* as recklessness. After visiting Urbino, the site of the conversations immortalized in *The Book of the Courtier*, Yeats wrote in his 1907 essay 'Poetry and Tradition' that Castiglione thought 'recklessness' a necessary attribute of the courtier. In the same essay, he remarked that, after the 'merely necessary' is established, a 'touch of extravagance' will engender 'the freedom of self-delight'. William Pollexfen's reckless and extravagant courage embodied the wasteful virtues that earn the sun.

Shortly after Yeats turned seven in the summer of 1872, he became a member of his grandfather's household when his father John Butler Yeats ('JBY') moved to London in an attempt to establish himself as a painter. The young Yeats, his mother, and his siblings lived with William and Elizabeth Pollexfen in Sligo for the next twenty-eight months, a critical period in the blossoming of the future poet's imagination. While living with their grandparents, the Yeats children would visit their cousins, aunts and uncles at their holiday homes at Rosses Point. The Yeats siblings went on to maintain connections with Sligo over the course of their lives. David Fitzpatrick's essay 'Sligo' estimates that Yeats spent 'perhaps seven years all told' in Sligo.

Writing in a draft memoir completed when he was about fifty years old, Yeats wrote, 'In a sense Sligo has always been my home'. His brother Jack lived in Sligo from ages eight through sixteen. Roy Foster's landmark *W.B. Yeats: A Life* concludes that Sligo was 'the world Jack Yeats drew upon for his art, and it formed the imagination of all his siblings too'.

Overleaf: *Reveries Over Childhood and Youth* (Cuala Press, 1915) with separately bound accompanying plates

REVERIES OVER CHILDHOOD AND YOUTH BY WILLIAM BUTLER YEATS

REVERIES OVER CHILDHOOD AND YOUTH BY WILLIAM BUTLER YEATS

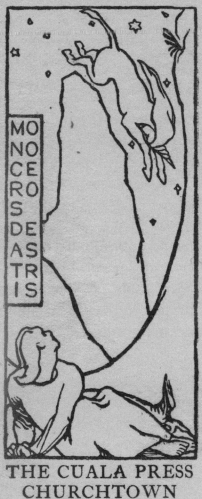

THE CUALA PRESS
CHURCHTOWN
DUNDRUM
MCMXV

2

Yeats's inscription of the aphorism that his Sligo grandfather
set his 'boyish lips to say'

Yeats gave permanent form to his connection with his Sligo ancestors by writing out this line in his own hand. Susan Howe memorably calls the experience of communing with the past through such bodily traces as 'the granting of grace in an ordinary room, in a secular time'.

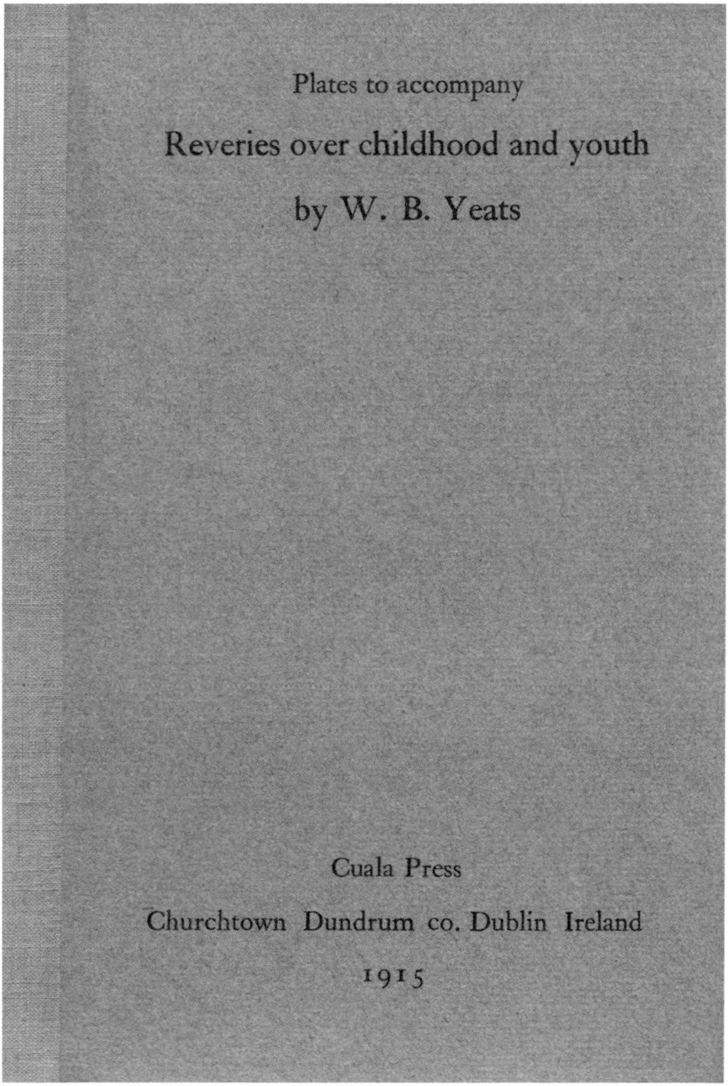

3

Plates to accompany

Reveries over childhood and youth

by W. B. Yeats

Cuala Press

Churchtown Dundrum co. Dublin Ireland

1915

This separately bound book contains illustrations that highlight particularly memorable aspects of Yeats's youth.

Yeats's reveries over his youth emphasize the importance of the people and places of Sligo. He highlights a comment by his father that identifies the Pollexfens of Sligo and the town's sea cliffs as the source of his poetic power. The 'only eulogy that turns my head', he says, is his father's comment: "We have ideas and no passions, but by marriage with a Pollexfen we have given a tongue to the sea cliffs'".

Yeats drove home the contrasting influences of his voluble father and his silent mother by including two antithetical images in the plates that accompany *Reveries*. One is his father's self-portrait in which JBY focuses his gaze on the reader. The other is his father's sketch of his mother looking vaguely into the distance.

Mrs Yeats
from a drawing by J. B. Yeats made in 1867

John Butler Yeats
from a watercolour drawing by himself

Because we know Yeats through his words, the influence of JBY (the tongue) is easily discerned, but the silence of Susan Pollexfen Yeats (the sea cliffs) remains a hidden force. Read in conjunction with a comment in the text of *Reveries*, the third image in the plates subtly illuminates the mysterious power of Pollexfen silence to elicit Yeatsian speech. The image is the Metal Man who dominates Jack's painting *Memory Harbour.*

"MEMORY HARBOUR" is the village of Rosses Point, but with the distances shortened and the houses run together as in an old-fashioned panoramic map. The man on the pedestal in the middle of the river is "the metal man," and he points to where the water is deep enough for ships. The coffin, cross-bones, skull, and loaf at the point of the headland are to remind one of the sailor who was buried there by a ship's crew in a hurry not to miss the tide. As they were not sure if he was really dead they buried with him a loaf as the story runs.

W. B. Y.

Yeats's note to the plates explains, 'The man on the pedestal in the middle of the river is "the metal man," and he points to where the water is deep enough for ships'. He was cast in 1819 by Thomas Kirke in London, and has a twin in Tramore, County Waterford. Courageous guide to safe navigation around potential peril, the Metal Man personifies the spirit of the silent and fierce old man whose courage in diving into the harbour under the Metal Man's watchful eyes set Yeats's youthful lips to say, 'Only the wasteful virtues earn the sun'.

The Metal Man's evocation of Pollexfen silence – transmitted from the poet's grandfather through his silent mother – explains why Yeats writes in *Reveries* that when he looks at *Memory Harbour*, 'I am full of disquiet and excitement, and I am melancholy because I have not made more and better verses'. In other words, at age fifty, he had not yet given sufficient tongue to the sea cliffs. Twenty-three years later he would write the magnificent 'Long-legged Fly', which asserts three times that history's transformative moments occur when 'mind moves upon silence'. Evoking his mother's vague expression in JBY's sketch, Yeats is careful to note that as Caesar prepares to save civilization, he pauses with 'His eyes fixed upon nothing' as 'His mind moves upon silence':

> That civilisation may not sink,
> Its great battle lost,
> Quiet the dog, tether the pony

To a distant post;
Our master Caesar is in the tent
Where the maps are spread,
His eyes fixed upon nothing,
A hand upon his head.

Like a long-legged fly upon the stream
His mind moves upon silence.

Yeats leaves no room for doubt that artistic creation
also proceeds from silence:

There on that scaffolding reclines
Michael Angelo.
With no more sound than the mice make
His hand moves to and fro.

Like a long-legged fly upon the stream
His mind moves upon silence.

Overleaf: Jack B. Yeats, *Life in the West of Ireland* (Maunsel and
Company Ltd, 1912): cover and frontispiece

LIFE IN THE WEST
OF IRELAND

DRAWN AND PAINTED
BY JACK B. YEATS

THE METAL MAN

4

The Metal Man captured the imagination of the entire Yeats family. In addition to being written about and mentioned in the midst of the work of JBY and both his sons in *Reveries Over Childhood and Youth*, the Metal Man features prominently in Jack B. Yeats's *Life in the West of Ireland*. The Metal Man spoke so powerfully to the family's collective memory of Sligo that Jack sketched him on an envelope sent to his sister Susan Mary, known as Lily and addressed here as Lilly, and she put Jack's drawing of the Metal Man on her bookplate.

Jack B. Yeats, envelope with sketch addressed to Lily Yeats, 1906
© Estate of Jack B. Yeats, DACS London / IVARO Dublin, 2023
Image courtesy Digital Collections, The Library of Trinity College Dublin

Jack B. Yeats, Lily Yeats bookplate (c. 1905) © Estate of Jack B. Yeats,
DACS London / IVARO Dublin, 2023

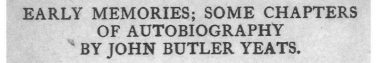

5

EARLY MEMORIES; SOME CHAPTERS
OF AUTOBIOGRAPHY
BY JOHN BUTLER YEATS.

THE CUALA PRESS
CHURCHTOWN
DUNDRUM
MCMXXIII

This memoir contains JBY's explanation of the compliment that so pleased his son. The elder Yeats describes the 'solitariness' that was 'characteristic of the whole [Pollexfen] family', whereas 'I myself am eagerly communicative, and when my son first revealed to me his gift [for] verse, "Ah!" I said, "Behold, I have given a tongue to the sea-cliffs."'

In addition to this book's interesting conjunction of father and son, it also embodies the artistry of JBY's daughter Elizabeth in various ways. The title page contains her line drawing showing a lone tree against an Irish landscape, which became Cuala's press mark in 1925, and the colophon at the rear of the book provides, in distinctive red colour, the context that the book was 'Finished in the last week of July nineteen hundred and twenty three, the second year of THE IRISH FREE STATE.'

Here ends 'EARLY MEMORIES: SOME CHAPTERS OF AUTOBIOGRAPHY BY JOHN BUTLER YEATS' Five hundred copies of this book have been printed and published by Elizabeth C. Yeats at the Cuala Press, Churchtown, Dundrum, in the County of Dublin Ireland. Finished in the last week of July ninteen hundred and twenty three, the second year of THE IRISH FREE STATE.

John Butler Yeats, *Early Memories* (Cuala Press, 1923):
title page and colophon

All of the beautiful Cuala Press books reflect the work of Elizabeth Yeats as publisher. Both she and her sister Susan Mary Yeats were pioneering Irish artists and artisans. Both spent part of their childhood in Sligo, and both became associated with the Arts and Crafts movement through association with William Morris's daughter May. They brought the Arts and Crafts aesthetic to an enterprise in which both were involved, Dun Emer Industries, the publishing arm of which eventually became the Cuala Press.

Through Elizabeth's connection with May Morris and her father William she became acquainted with Emery Walker, whose famous lecture on 'Letterpress Printing and Illustration' inspired William Morris to establish the Kelmscott Press. On Walker's advice, Elizabeth Yeats took a month-long course of classes in printing at the Women's Printing Society in London, and eventually applied Walker's principles in publishing the Cuala books. She acquired an Albion hand press similar to that used at the Kelmscott Press and, again on Walker's advice, purchased and used a font of Caslon Old Style type in 14 point size.

As Yeats's son Michael later wrote, 'The press was from the start a Yeats family affair, and, besides my aunts, my father, my uncle, and my grandfather were all involved in its affairs, in one respect or another'. The Cuala Press books are a lasting amalgam of Sligo and the Arts and Crafts movement.

6

The essay 'Drumcliff and Rosses' in the first edition of *The Celtic Twilight* proclaims, 'Drumcliff and Rosses were, are, and ever shall be, please heaven! places of unearthly resort. I have lived near by them and in them, time after time, and have gathered thus many a crumb of faery lore.' In *Reveries Over Childhood and Youth* WBY credits his uncle George Pollexfen's servant Mary Battle, who 'had the second sight', as a principal source of his knowledge of faery lore. 'Much of my "Celtic Twilight"', he writes, 'is but her daily speech.'

Overleaf: *The Celtic Twilight* (Lawrence and Bullen, 1893): title page and frontispiece containing reproduction of John Butler Yeats's *The Last Gleeman*

THE LAST GLEEMAN.

THE CELTIC TWILIGHT.

MEN AND WOMEN, DHOULS AND FAERIES.

BY

W. B. YEATS.

WITH A FRONTISPIECE BY J. B. YEATS.

LONDON:

LAWRENCE AND BULLEN,

16, HENRIETTA ST., COVENT GARDEN.

1893.

7

Poems (T. Fisher Unwin, 1899)

This book, beautifully designed by Althea Gyles, contains Yeats's iconic poem 'The Lake Isle of Innisfree':

I will arise and go now, and go to Innisfree,
And a small cabin build there, of clay and wattles
    made;
Nine bean-rows will I have there, a hive for the
    honey-bee,
And live alone in the bee-loud glade.

And I shall have some peace there, for peace
    comes dropping slow,
Dropping from the veils of the morning to where
    the cricket sings;
There midnight's all a glimmer, and noon a
    purple glow,
And evening full of the linnet's wings.

I will arise and go now, for always night and day
I hear lake water lapping with low sounds by the
    shore;
While I stand on the roadway, or on the pavements
    grey,
I hear it in the deep heart's core.

The magnetic attraction of Sligo as a place of writing is nowhere better expressed. The poem is a good example of Seamus Heaney's first category – poems in which the poet gives voice to the spirit of the region. Yeats wrote that the sound of bubbling water on a busy

London street reminded him of Innisfree, and kindled his desire to live there in imitation of Henry David Thoreau, who famously 'went to the woods because [he] wished to live deliberately'. Yeats was twenty-five years old when this poem was first published. The next poem in the collection, 'The Fiddler of Dooney', another example of Heaney's first category, was published two years later.

This Ordnance Survey map shows the proximity of the famous Lake Isle to Sligo:

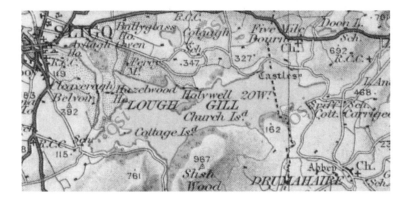

While the simplicity of the poem contrasts with the gilt-stamped Rosicrucian imagery on the cover, the frontispiece portrait of the author by Jack B. Yeats reinforces the Yeats–Sligo connection.

Poems (T. Fisher Unwin, 1899): frontispiece portrait
of WBY by Jack B. Yeats

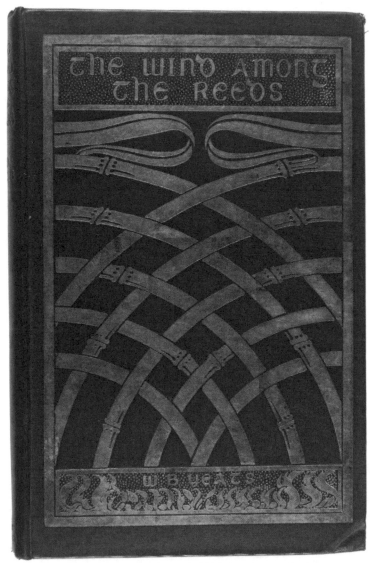

8

The Wind Among the Reeds (Elkin Matthews, 1899)

Another iconic cover by Althea Gyles graces the volume containing a much-loved evocation of Sligo, 'The Fiddler of Dooney', in which Yeats also imposes a vision on the place. As Roy Foster points out in *W.B. Yeats: A Life, I: The Apprentice Mage*, the subversive fiddler prefers books of song to priestly texts, and goes first though Peter's gate, thus suggesting that art trumps religion.

When I play on my fiddle in Dooney,
Folk dance like a wave of the sea;
My cousin is priest in Kilvarnet,
My brother in Mocharabuiee.

I passed my brother and cousin:
They read in their books of prayer;
I read in my book of songs
I bought at the Sligo fair.

When we come at the end of time
To Peter sitting in state,
He will smile on the three old spirits,
But call me first through the gate;

For the good are always the merry,
Save by an evil chance,
And the merry love to fiddle,
And the merry love to dance:

And when the folk there spy me,
They will all come up to me,

With 'Here is the fiddler of Dooney!'
And dance like a wave of the sea.

The other-worldly aura of 'The Lake Isle of Innisfree' and 'The Fiddler of Dooney' accords perfectly with the mood of the Althea Gyles covers for the volumes in which the poems appear. Yeats wrote of Gyles in the December 1898 issue of *The Dome*: 'her inspiration is the wave of a hidden tide that is flowing through many minds in many places, creating a new religious art and poetry'. Yeats found what T.S. Eliot would later call an 'objective correlative' for those hidden tides in the lake water lapping on Inisfree and the swaying listeners to the fiddler of Dooney who 'dance like a wave of the sea'.

9

The Winding Stair and Other Poems (Macmillan, 1933)

This memorable design by T. Sturge Moore graces the cover of the volume containing 'In Memory of Eva Gore-Booth and Constance Markiewicz', a poem in which the sixty-two year old poet both pictures an aspect of Sligo and imposes his view on it. He begins by evoking the Sligo he shared with the Gore-Booth sisters in his youth, then moves to a place of the mind featuring a disapproving verbal portrait of their subsequent lives. The two girls in silk kimonos, who once basked in the light of evening at Lissadell, have become shadows. The enemy here is time, and the poem ends with an explosive call to obliterate it.

> The light of evening, Lissadell,
> Great windows open to the south,
> Two girls in silk kimonos, both
> Beautiful, one a gazelle.
> But a raving autumn shears
> Blossom from the summer's wreath;
> The older is condemned to death,
> Pardoned, drags out lonely years
> Conspiring among the ignorant.
> I know not what the younger dreams –
> Some vague Utopia – and she seems,
> When withered old and skeleton-gaunt,
> An image of such politics.
> Many a time I think to seek
> One or the other out and speak
> Of that old Georgian mansion, mix

Pictures of the mind, recall
That table and the talk of youth,
Two girls in silk kimonos, both
Beautiful, one a gazelle.

Dear shadows, now you know it all,
All the folly of a fight
With a common wrong or right.
The innocent and the beautiful
Have no enemy but time;
Arise and bid me strike a match
And strike another till time catch;
Should the conflagration climb,
Run till all the sages know.
We the great gazebo built,
They convicted us of guilt;
Bid me strike a match and blow.

Yeats's draft memoir evokes the Sligo inhabited by him and the Gore-Booths in their youth:

Con Gore-Booth all through my later boyhood had been romantic to me ...

She had often passed me on horseback, going or coming from some hunt, and was acknowledged beauty of the county. I heard now and then [of] some tom-boyish feat or of her reckless riding, but the general impression was always that she was respected and admired ...

I was at once in closer sympathy with her sister, Eva, whose delicate, gazelle-like beauty, reflected a mind far more subtle and distinguished. Eva was for a couple of happy weeks my close friend, and I told her all of my unhappiness in love; indeed so close at once that I nearly said to her, as William Blake said to Catherine Boucher, 'You pity me, there[fore] I love you.' 'But no', I thought, this house would never accept so penniless a suitor ... I threw the Tarot, and when the Fool came up, which means that nothing at all would happen, I turned my mind away.

In 'On a Political Prisoner', after denouncing the politics of the mature Constance Markiewicz, Yeats brings the youthful Con Gore-Booth back to life in the poem's concluding stanzas:

> She that but little patience knew,
> From childhood on, had now so much
> A grey gull lost its fear and flew
> Down to her cell and there alit,
> And there endured her fingers' touch
> And from her fingers ate its bit.
>
> Did she in touching that lone wing
> Recall the years before her mind
> Became a bitter, an abstract thing,
> Her thought some popular enmity:
> Blind and leader of the blind
> Drinking the foul ditch where they lie?
>
> When long ago I saw her ride
> Under Ben Bulben to the meet,

The beauty of her country-side
With all youth's lonely wildness stirred,
She seemed to have grown clean and sweet
Like any rock-bred, sea-borne bird:

Sea-borne, or balanced in the air
When first it sprang out of the nest
Upon some lofty rock to stare
Upon the cloudy canopy,
While under its storm-beaten breast
Cried out the hollows of the sea.

10

New Poems (Cuala Press, 1939): title page signed by WBY

Sligo was a vivid presence in Yeats's mental landscape from first to last. In a poem in this volume, 'Are You Content?', published just months before his death, WBY links himself to his ancestors, especially those hailing from Sligo:

> I call on those that call me son,
> Grandson, or great-grandson,
> On uncles, aunts, great-uncles or great-aunts,
> To judge what I have done.
> Have I, that put it into words,
> Spoilt what old loins have sent?
> Eyes spiritualised by death can judge,
> I cannot, but I am not content.
>
> He that in Sligo at Drumcliff
> Set up the old stone Cross,
> That red-headed rector in County Down,
> A good man on a horse,
> Sandymount Corbets, that notable man
> Old William Pollexfen,
> The smuggler Middleton, Butlers far back,
> Half legendary men.

This poem picks up where Yeats left off at age forty-nine in *Responsibilities*, but in a different posture. In the earlier poem, he specifically sought the pardon of his ancestors, his 'old fathers', as he called them; now he simply submits to their judgment on his life.

'Old William Pollexfen', the most memorable ancestor in *Responsibilities*, is given pride of place in this poem as 'that notable man', thus continuing the elevated status reflected in the fact that the opening lines of 'In Memory of Alfred Pollexfen', written in 1916, were devoted to 'old William Pollexfen'.

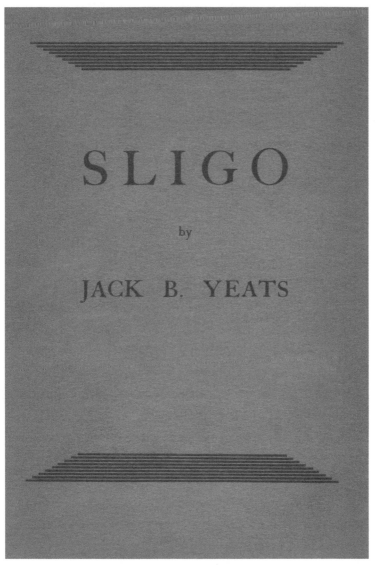

11

Jack B. Yeats, *Sligo* (Wishart & Company, 1930)

The colour and excitement of life in Sligo and its harbour stirred Jack B. Yeats's imagination so powerfully that its beaches, boats, boxers and circuses animate countless paintings and drawings. His book *Sligo* evokes the town in words.

After reading *Sligo*, Jack's brother insightfully situated its style in the fashion of James Joyce. He wrote to Jack on 18 July 1930:

> It is the best of talk & the best of writing and at the top of a fine fashion – I think of James Joyce's associations. 'My new book is about the night & I have had to put language asleep' he said to me a few days ago.

Joyce had famously told his friend Frank Budgen that *Ulysses,* his book about daylight Dublin, would 'give a picture of Dublin so complete that if the city one day suddenly disappeared from the earth, it could be reconstructed out of my book'. Jack B. Yeats's *Sligo* creates a record of life in Sligo, albeit in a less exhaustive manner. Language sleeps in *Finnegans Wake* and snoozes in Jack's *Sligo* as it gently evokes the town's exciting characters. Jack's writing about the circus in *Sligo* is a good example of the texture of the book. The painter–writer conjures 'three men standing on a sandy shore with a Circus tent pitched on the sands and around them Circus wagons and disillusioned skew bald horses hiding their amusement'. He tells us that he 'heard these beings talking of the great Circus men of the past, the Ginnetts, the Lloyds, the Johnnie Pattersons of the days of old ...'

Jack's *Johnnie Patterson Singing 'Bridget Donoghue'* is part of the Niland Collection (created by co-founder of the Yeats Summer School, Nora Niland) at Sligo's The Model gallery.

Johnnie Patterson's afterlife in the words, sketches and paintings of Jack B. Yeats validate Jack's observation in *Sligo* about the long life of grand names in the popular memory:

> Grand names, like hand-sewn boots, disintegrate very slowly. You'll find them crinkled, but undefeated, lying on the slob lands of the world: hurled from Land to Land like old skulls by the youthful Treasure hunters who comb those dusty beaches for old nails, and an odd dust-heap diamond. Sitting by a boxing ring it cheers up the ancients when the announcer rings out the name of some old timer, now fat, or weazened, acting as a second to the opening buds of this night. And those ancients lick their old lips when the name of Jimmy this or Jack that gets a call of 'Ho Ho' from someone far sunk in the back of the hall: someone who does not forget.

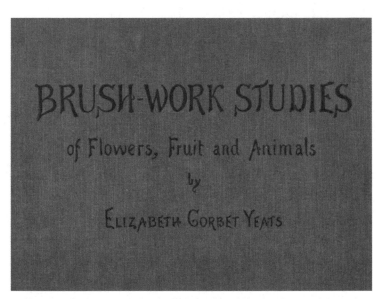

12

Elizabeth Corbet Yeats, *Brush Work Studies of Flowers, Fruit and Animals*
(George Philip & Son, 1898)

As mentioned in chapter 5, the beautiful Cuala books in the Yeats in Sligo Collection reflect Elizabeth's distinguished career as a publisher of hand-printed books. The book pictured here demonstrates her accomplishments as an artist.

PLATE XIV.

LAST POEMS AND TWO PLAYS
BY WILLIAM BUTLER YEATS.

THE CUALA PRESS
DUBLIN IRELAND
MCMXXXIX

THE MAN AND THE ECHO
MAN
In a cleft that's christened Alt
Under broken stone I halt
At the bottom of a pit
That broad noon has never lit,
And shout a secret to the stone.
All that I have said and done,
Now that I am old and ill,
Turns into a question till
I lie awake night after night
And never get the answers right.
Did that play of mine send out
Certain men the English shot?
Did words of mine put too great strain
On that woman's reeling brain?
Could my spoken words have checked
That whereby a house lay wrecked?
And all seems evil until I
Sleepless would lie down and die.

27

Last Poems and Two Plays by William Butler Yeats (Cuala Press, 1939):
title page and excerpt from 'The Man and the Echo' on page 27

The title of this Cuala Press volume signals its function as the poet's final testament. Significantly, two of the volume's poems implant the poet as a permanent part of the Sligo landscape.

In 'The Man and the Echo', written just months before Yeats's death, the Man propounds a series of questions in a rocky cleft on the slope of Knocknarea, just west of Sligo town. The Echo answers by echoing the final word or words of the question.

For example, the Echo's answer to the question propounded at the bottom of the image on the previous page is 'Lie down and die'. After another such question and echoing answer the Man asks, 'Shall we in that great night rejoice?'

Because the rocky voice of the Echo may be expected to return the speaker's last word, his leading question invites the answer 'Rejoice'. The Echo may thus be expected to proclaim that in that great night that follows death, we shall rejoice.

Since Yeats hasn't finished this process, the echo has not yet reached his ears, and his distracted state seems ominous. Nonetheless, the word 'rejoice' has been launched and its expected rebound justifies Seamus Heaney's conclusion that the poem manages 'to pronounce a final Yes'. Moreover, as Heaney puts it, 'the Yes is valuable because we can say of it what Karl Barth said of the enormous Yes at the centre of Mozart's music, that it has weight and significance because it overpowers and contains a No'.

The Man has felt the pull of the urge to lie down and die, but has mastered the art of keeping going. His resolute, unflinching attitude reflects the lingering influence of William Pollexfen. As he embraces the end of his life, Yeats both expresses the voice of Sligo in Rocky Face and imposes his own view on Sligo in the voice of the Man.

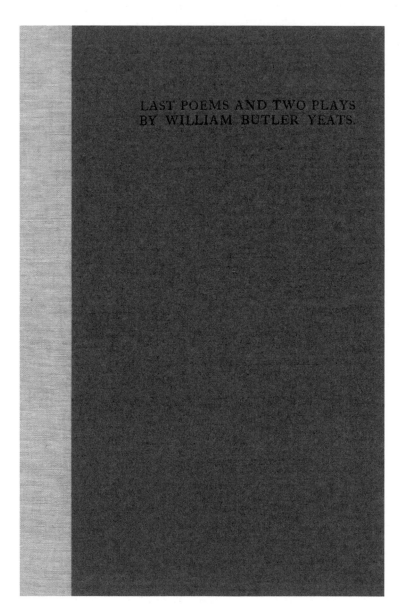

LAST POEMS AND TWO PLAYS
BY WILLIAM BUTLER YEATS.

VI

Under bare Ben Bulben's head
In Drumcliffe churchyard Yeats is laid.
An ancestor was rector there
Long years ago, a church stands near,
By the road an ancient cross.
No marble, no conventional phrase;
On limestone quarried near the spot
By his command these words are cut:

4

Cast a cold eye
On life, on death.
Horseman pass by!
                    September 4th 1938.

Last Poems and Two Plays by William Butler Yeats (Cuala Press, 1939):
cover and stanza VI of 'Under Ben Bulben' on pages 4-5

W.B. Yeats gravestone in Drumcliffe churchyard with Ben Bulben in the background. Alain Le Garsmeur, *W.B. Yeats: Images of Ireland* / Alamy stock photo

What could be a more powerful instance of what Seamus Heaney calls a poet's 'dominating relationship to the physical world' than Yeats's declaration in this volume of last poems that 'Under bare Ben Bulben's head / In Drumcliffe churchyard Yeats is laid'? Sligo thus also becomes the beginning of Yeats's post-life journey. Yeats localized that journey by commenting that his poem 'Sailing to Byzantium' symbolizes 'the spiritual life as a journey to Byzantium'. Thus the dominating force of Yeats's declaration that he is buried under Ben Bulben is brilliantly captured in William Gass's assertion that Yeats 'sets Byzantium down in Sligo'.

There is a sense in which Drumcliffe churchyard became the site of Yeats's grave the moment the line so declaring was written. It follows that inquiry into whether the corpse interred in France in 1939 for transfer after the end of World War II actually made it to Drumcliffe is beside the point. In his poem, Yeats permanently fixed his resting place in Drumcliffe, a place whose significance is emphatically declared: 'An ancestor was rector there'. By the performative act of writing these lines Yeats both identified his final resting place and also linked himself in the human chain with Reverend John Yeats, who was Rector at Drumcliffe from 1811 to 1846.

In 'Under Ben Bulben' Yeats reminds us that his Yeats ancestors, like his Pollexfen old fathers of *Responsibilities*, are an enduring part of Sligo history.

Acknowledgments

Thank you to the people of Sligo who have welcomed me warmly since I first attended the Yeats Summer School – the Fourth Annual – in 1963. The opening ceremony that year in neighbouring Drumcliffe Church was magical. Even a fledgling student knew the ringing lines in which Yeats declared,

> Under bare Ben Bulben's head
> In Drumcliffe churchyard Yeats is laid.
> An ancestor was rector there ...

I could not have foreseen that fifty-six years later I would have the honour of delivering the opening address at the Sixtieth Yeats Summer School to an audience at Drumcliffe Church that included the great-great-great-granddaughters of the ancestor referred to in Yeats's poem, Reverend John Yeats, who was Rector at Drumcliffe from 1811 to 1846. The feeling that night of being a link in a human chain of 208 years was one I'll never forget.

Thank you to the Yeats family for their generous welcome and assistance. Early in my journey as a Yeats scholar, Michael Yeats turned up at a lecture I was giving, chatted amiably afterwards, and kindly answered letters asking about his father's papers. Michael and his wife Gráinne often conversed with me over lunch at the annual Autumn Gathering at Coole Park, County Galway. Michael and I sat together at the opening of the National Library of Ireland's Yeats exhibition in 2006, not long before his death. His sister, Anne Yeats, was wonderfully generous, often welcoming me to her home to browse her father's books. Caitríona Yeats's interest and support continues her family's welcoming tradition. I am grateful for her friendship.

Thank you to the community of Yeats scholars who are always ready to help, and in particular to Roy Foster and Jim Flannery for embracing the idea of this book and suggesting ways of improving it. Thank you to Irish poets for their ideas and friendship, particularly Paula Meehan and Theo Dorgan for their welcome to this book and its author.

Thank you to Antony Farrell, publisher of Lilliput Press, for his ideas and encouragement and for making a book in Lilliput's distinctive and elegant style; to Stephen Reid and everyone at Lilliput for making it happen; and to Marsha Swan and Iota Books for extraordinary cover design and typesetting that delights the eye.

Thank you to Digital Collections, The Library of Trinity College Dublin, the University of Dublin (Jennifer Doyle) and the National Gallery of Ireland Library and Archives (Sean Mooney) for efficient and courteous assistance with digital images.

The author greatly appreciates the work of Yeats Society Sligo in curating, with the assistance of the National Library of Ireland, a 'Sligo in Yeats' exhibit that will feature many of the items described in this book and will be available to the public at the Society's building.

Further Reading

This book focuses primarily on material donated to Yeats Society Sligo by the author, and does not attempt a full account of Yeats and Sligo. Roy Foster's 'The Yeats Family and Sligo' (details below) provides a comprehensive and concise history.

Kevin Connolly, *Arise and Go* (The O'Brien Press, 2019)

Kevin Connolly, *Yeats and Sligo* (Brandon, 2010)

Anne Margaret Daniel, 'Homecoming: Yeats and Sligo' in Declan J. Foley (ed.), *Yeats 150* (Lilliput Press, 2016)

David Fitzpatrick, 'Sligo' in David Holdeman and Ben Levitas (eds), *W.B. Yeats in Context* (Cambridge University Press, 2010)

R.F. Foster, 'The Yeats Family and Sligo' in Kieran O'Conor (ed.), *Sligo History and Society: Interdisciplinary Essays on the History of an Irish County* (Dublin, forthcoming 2024)

R.F. Foster, *W.B. Yeats: A Life, I: The Apprentice Mage* (Oxford University Press, 1997)

R.F. Foster, *W.B. Yeats: A Life, II: The Arch-Poet* (Oxford University Press, 2003)

Seamus Heaney, *The Place of Writing* (Scholars Press, 1989)

Seamus Heaney, 'Joy or Night: Last Things in the Poetry of W.B. Yeats and Phillip Larkin' in *Finders Keepers: Selected Prose 1971–2001* (Faber and Faber, 2002)

Sheelah Kirby, *The Yeats Country: A Guide to Places in the West of Ireland Associated with the Life and Writings of William Butler Yeats*, edited by Patrick Gallagher (Dolmen Press, 1962)

James P. McGarry, *Place Names in the Writings of William Butler Yeats*, edited by Edward Malins (Colin Smythe, 1976)

Liam Miller, *The Dun Emer Press, Later the Cuala Press*, with a preface by Michael B. Yeats (Dolmen Press, 1973)

William Murphy, *The Yeats Family and the Pollexfens of Sligo* (Dolmen Press, 1971)

Nora Niland, Secretary/Curator Sligo County Museum and Library, *Jack B Yeats and his Family* (Sligo, 1971)